THE BAND METHOD THAT TEACHES MUSIC READING

RHYTHM
MASTER

Supplemental Material

By

J.R. McEntyre
Coordinator of Music, Retired
Odessa Public Schools
Odessa, Texas

And

Harry H. Haines
Music Department Chairman
West Texas State University
Canyon, Texas

Horn Fingering Chart

NOTE: Those students using a double horn (F-B flat) should, as a habit, play all notes G (second line) and lower on the F horn (thumb valve open) and all notes G Sharp (second line) and higher on the B flat horn (thumb valve closed).

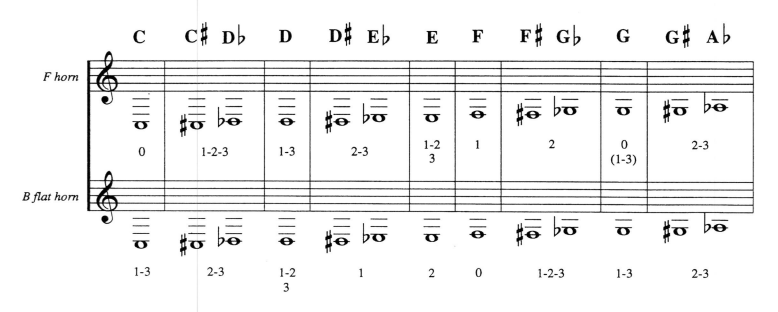

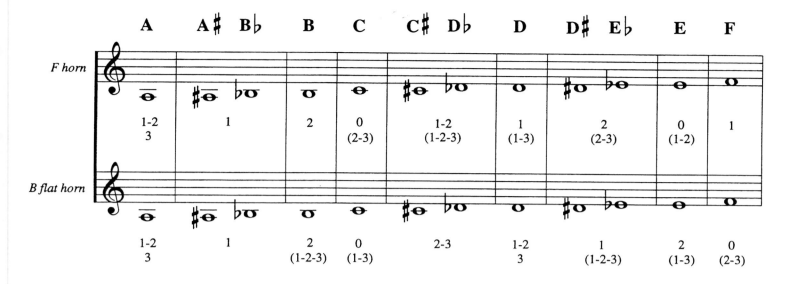

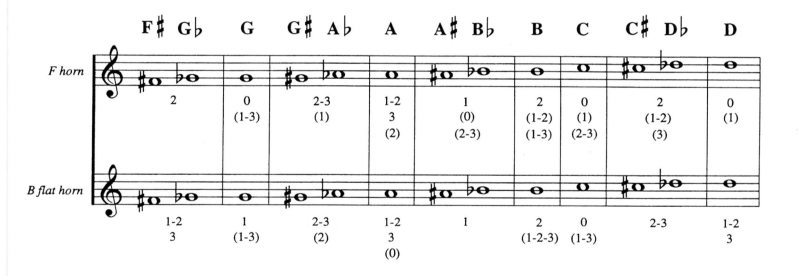

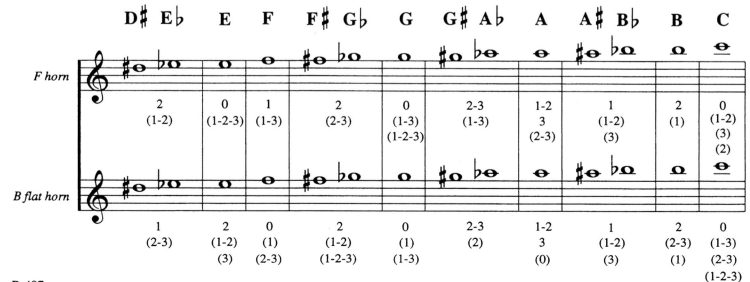

Preliminary Lesson
The Most Important Lesson!

Some aspects of learning to play a band instrument are best learned without an instruction book. This is especially true of the very first stages such as 1) putting the instrument together, 2) learning correct posture and position, and 3) producing the sound. Also, an understanding of a few basic music symbols will be a great help in beginning to read a method book. The authors believe that best results will be achieved if the teacher approaches this lesson using a Suzuki-like presentation. The basis should be rote teaching using much imitation and repetition.

The **Conductor's Guide** contains specific information about each instrument and suggestions from a master teacher for introducing the embouchure.

How long should you spend on a **Preliminary Lesson**? Teaching situations vary but most successful beginning band classes we know get better results when they spend four or five hours on this material. At a minimum, tone production and articulation should be established to a point where students are able to consistently produce the pitch for their first note in **LESSON 1**.

1 Start with the mouthpiece only. Learn to make a buzzing sound. Vary the pitch level. Try to make a high buzz, then a low buzz. Imitate your teacher. A great many later problems can be avoided by preliminary buzzing on the brass mouthpiece.

2 Work on correct posture. Pay careful attention to your teacher's instructions. Air is the lifeblood of your sound. No one can play an instrument well unless he/she has good breath support. Good posture is an acquired habit and the time to start is the first day.

3 Put the instrument together properly and learn to hold it correctly. Practice this many times until you can do it well. Instruments may look strong but they are really quite delicate and are easily damaged. Each student must learn how to care for his/her instrument and there will never be a better time than now.

4 Produce a characteristic sound. To do this requires much repetition. Every person learns to play an instrument by the "trial and error" method. One of the essential aspects of success is to "try" enough times to give the method a chance for learning to occur. Repetition, correct instruction, and constant, intelligent analysis are the three primary aspects of learning to play an instrument. The most important of these is (you guessed it) _repetition_! You must go over and over your basic sound always trying to make it better.

5 Practice articulation. Start the sound with your tongue and release with your breath. Learning how to begin and end a tone and coordinate the use of your tongue should be a major goal of this **Preliminary Lesson**.

6 Finally, every student must learn a few basic music symbols before he/she can begin to read music. **LESSON 1** will be much easier if you know the musical terms below. Throughout this book, the red, numbered flags refer to the **Index of Musical Terms** found on the back cover.

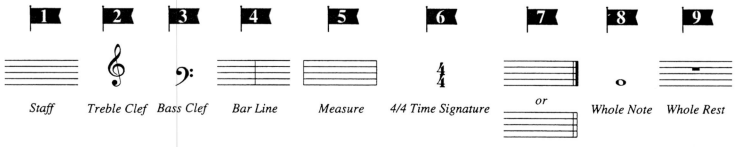

| Staff | Treble Clef | Bass Clef | Bar Line | Measure | 4/4 Time Signature | or | Whole Note | Whole Rest |

Double Bar

Horns Only

LESSON 1
The First Note

G (treble clef, whole note)

F horn: 0
Bb horn: 1

> **NEW** These "flag" symbols indicate something new. New notes are flagged as "NEW."
>
> **1** A numbered flag refers to the **Index of Musical Terms** on the back cover.

1 **The First Note** *Repeat many times.*

Good tone quality requires good breath support. You cannot become an outstanding player unless you have a supported sound.

Whole note.
Four counts in 4/4 time.

Whole rest.
Four counts in 4/4 time.

2 **Whole Notes and Whole Rests** *Count each line carefully. Count the rests silently.*

3 **Quarter Notes and Quarter Rests**

4 **Mixing It Up**

5 **Half Notes and Half Rests**

6 **All Kinds of Notes**

7 **All Kinds of Rests** *Write the counting on the lines below the staff.*

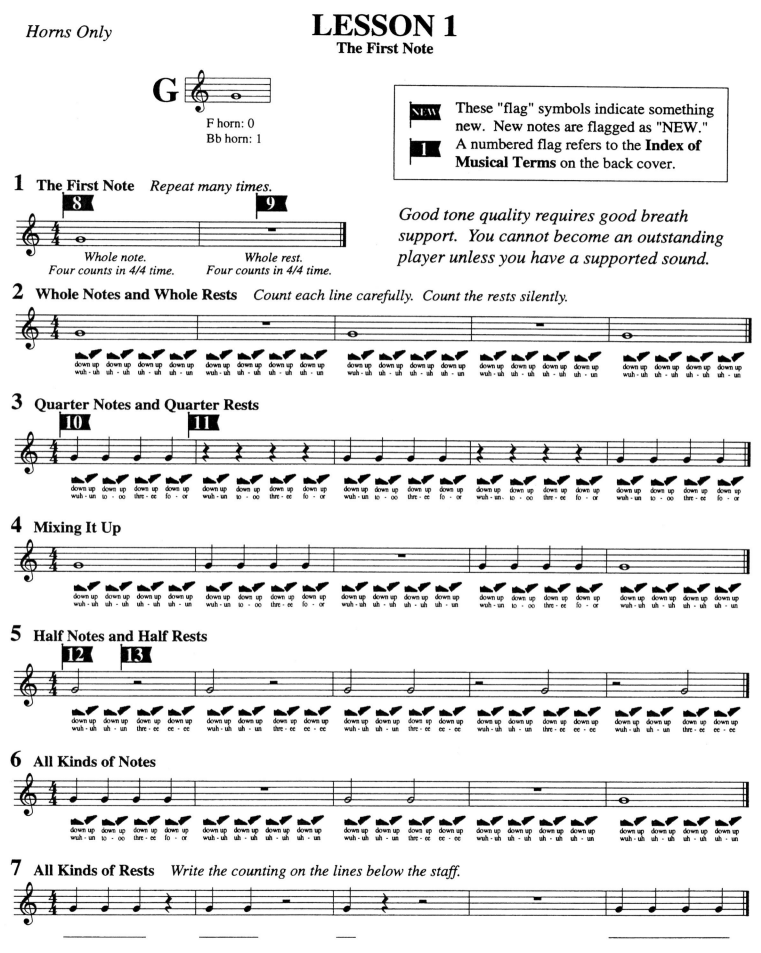

LESSON 1
The First Note

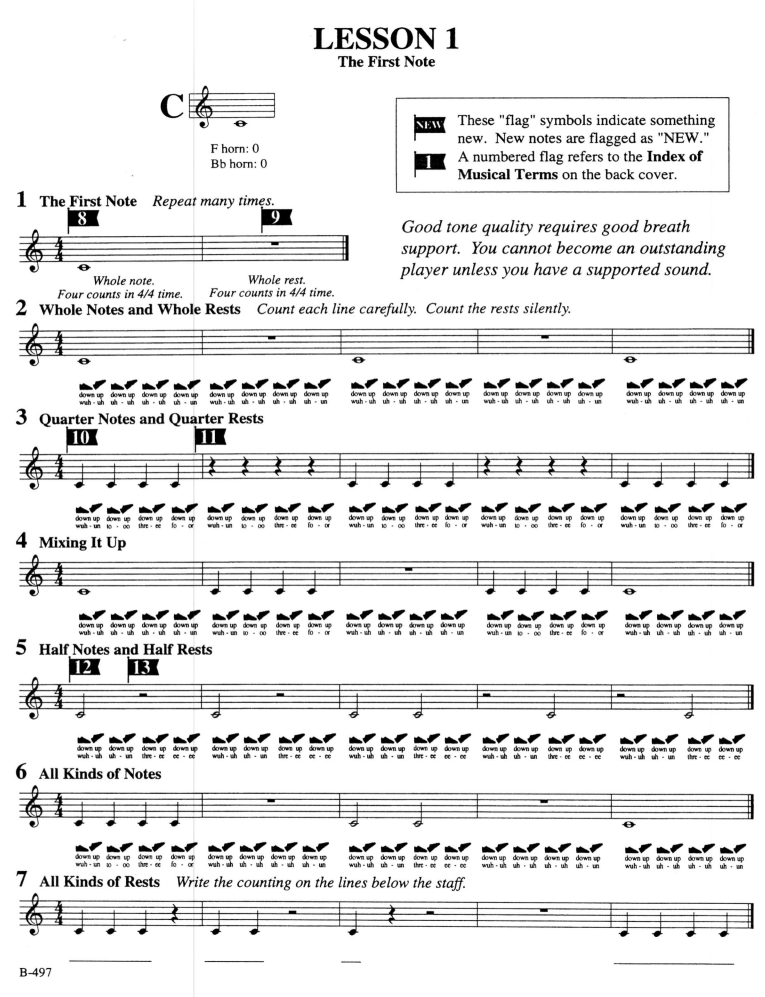

C

F horn: 0
Bb horn: 0

These "flag" symbols indicate something new. New notes are flagged as "NEW."

A numbered flag refers to the **Index of Musical Terms** on the back cover.

Good tone quality requires good breath support. You cannot become an outstanding player unless you have a supported sound.

1 The First Note   *Repeat many times.*

Whole note.
Four counts in 4/4 time.

Whole rest.
Four counts in 4/4 time.

2 Whole Notes and Whole Rests   *Count each line carefully. Count the rests silently.*

3 Quarter Notes and Quarter Rests

4 Mixing It Up

5 Half Notes and Half Rests

6 All Kinds of Notes

7 All Kinds of Rests   *Write the counting on the lines below the staff.*

Horns Only

LESSON 2
The Second Note

F horn: 1
Bb horn: 0

Tap your foot, count, and play every line.

8 **The Second Note** *Repeat many times.*

9 **Practice the New Note**

10 **Two-Note Song** *Write the counting on the lines below the staff.*

11 **First Duet** 14

12 **Duet Part**

13 **Quarter Notes and Quarter Rests**

14 **All Kinds of Notes**

15 **Who Will Play in the Rest?**

SUGGESTION: Start every class using Warm-up #1 on the last page of the book.

LESSON 2
The Second Note

SUGGESTION: Start every class using Warm-up #1 on the last page of the book.

Horns Only

LESSON 3
Three Notes

A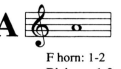

F horn: 1-2
Bb horn: 1-2

Good players can read music. Remember to tap your foot, count, and play every line.

16 The Third Note *Repeat many times.*

17 Three-Note Exercise

down up / wuh-uh   down up / uh-un   down up / thre-ee   down up / ee-ee   down up / wuh-uh   down up / uh-un   down up / thre-ee   down up / ee-ee   down up / wuh-uh   down up / uh-un   down up / thre-ee   down up / ee-ee   down up / wuh-uh   down up / uh-uh   down up / uh-uh   down up / uh-un

18 Echo Song

solo   class   solo   class   solo   class   solo   everyone

19 Duet: Hand Clappers

20 Duet: Finger Snappers

21 All Kinds of Notes

22 Who Will Play in the Rest (Again)?

23 Our First Song

LESSON 3
Three Notes

Horns Only

LESSON 4
The Eighth Note Lesson

*Always carry your instrument
case with the lid toward you.*

24 **Introducing Eighth Notes**

down up down up down up down up   down up down up down up down up down up down up down up down up   down up down up down up down up

25 **Eighth Notes and Quarter Notes**   *Write the counting on the lines below the staff.*

26 **Sneaky Second Count**

27 **Tricky Third Count**

28 **Freaky Fourth Count**

SPECIAL ASSIGNMENT: Before going to line 29, try to count and play the first measures of 25, 26, 27, and 28 straight down the page. Then do the second measures, then the third, etc. This is a great exercise in rhythm!

29 **All Mixed Up**

30 **Hot Cross Buns**

31 **Merrily We Speed Along**

LESSON 4
The Eighth Note Lesson

Always carry your instrument case with the lid toward you.

24 Introducing Eighth Notes

25 Eighth Notes and Quarter Notes   *Write the counting on the lines below the staff.*

26 Sneaky Second Count

27 Tricky Third Count

28 Freaky Fourth Count

SPECIAL ASSIGNMENT: Before going to line 29, try to count and play the first measures of 25, 26, 27, and 28 straight down the page. Then do the second measures, then the third, etc. This is a great exercise in rhythm!

29 All Mixed Up

30 Hot Cross Buns

31 Merrily We Speed Along

Horns Only

LESSON 5
The Fourth Note/Dotted Half Note Lesson

F horn: 0
Bb horn: 2

A dot after a note adds one half the value of that note.

B-497

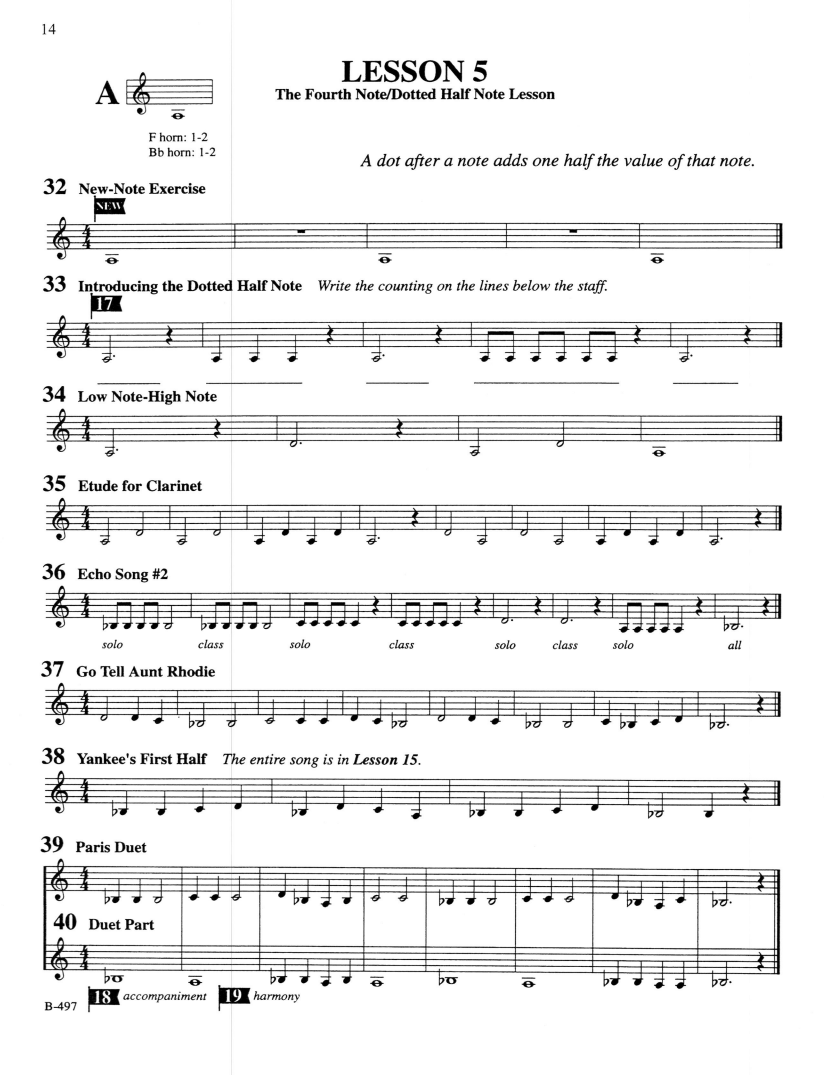

Horns Only

LESSON 6
The 2/4 Lesson

SUGGESTION: Expand your warm-up to include Warm-up #2 (and play it from memory).

LESSON 6
The 2/4 Lesson

SUGGESTION: Expand your warm-up to include Warm-up #2 (and play it from memory).

Rhythm Set #1
Eighth, Quarter, Half, and Whole Note Rhythms

18

LESSON 7
The 3/4 Lesson

Horns Only

flat

B♭

F horn: 1
Bb horn: 1

Good players are known for tone quality.
Are you playing with a supported sound?

49 High Note *Write the counting on the lines below the staff.*

How many counts?

50 Building Range *Go back to the beginning of this line.*

51 Eighth Note Etude *Go back to the first repeat sign.*

52 Variations on Line 51

53 Duet: Hand Clappers

54 Duet: Knee Slappers

55 Blow the Man Down

56 Hymn Tune

97

LESSON 7
The 3/4 Lesson

F horn: 2
Bb horn: 1

Good players are known for tone quality.
Are you playing with a supported sound?

49 High Note *Write the counting on the lines below the staff.*

How many counts?

50 Building Range *Go back to the beginning of this line.*

51 Eighth Note Etude *Go back to the first repeat sign.*

52 Variations on Line 51

53 Duet: Hand Clappers

54 Duet: Knee Slappers

55 Blow the Man Down

56 Hymn Tune

Horns Only

LESSON 8
Introducing the Tie

LESSON 8
Introducing the Tie

Horns Only

LESSON 9
The Dotted Quarter Lesson

Learn how to clean and care for your instrument properly.

67 Introducing the Dotted Quarter and Eighth Rest

Eighth notes are sometimes written with a single flag on the stem.

68 Another Way (To Introduce the Dotted Quarter and Eighth Rest)

69 Dotted Quarters Everywhere

70 Song with Dotted Quarter

71 America

72 Alma Mater

73 Careless Love

SUGGESTION: Add the first two measures of Warm-up #3 to your daily routine.

23

LESSON 9

The Dotted Quarter Lesson

Learn how to clean and care for your instrument properly.

F horn: 1-2
Bb horn: 2

67 Introducing the Dotted Quarter and Eighth Rest

Eighth notes are sometimes written with a single flag on the stem.

68 Another Way (To Introduce the Dotted Quarter and Eighth Rest)

69 Dotted Quarters Everywhere

70 Song with Dotted Quarter

71 America — NEW *If this note is too low, play the smaller note.*

72 Alma Mater

73 Careless Love

SUGGESTION: Add the first two measures of Warm-up #3 to your daily routine.

Rhythm Set #2
Dotted Quarter Rhythms

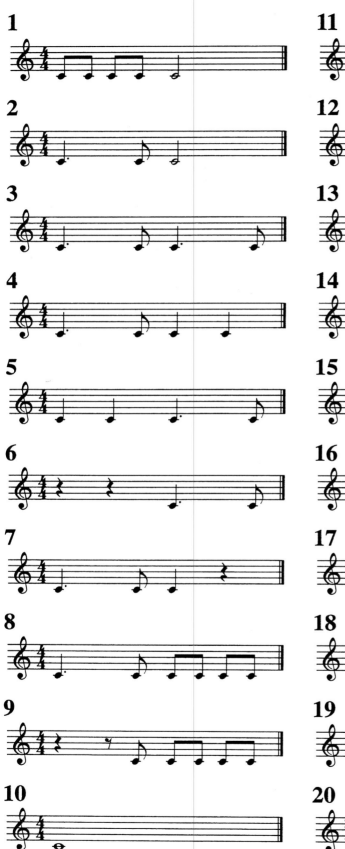

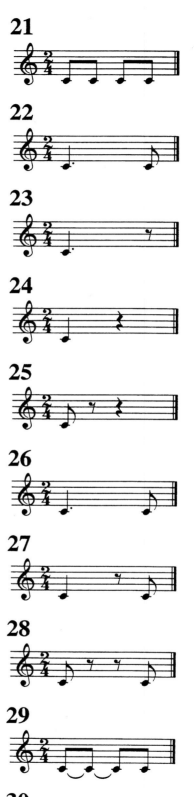

LESSON 10
Dotted Quarter Drill

Horns Only

You can tell how good players are by the way they look. Good players have good posture and instrument position.

LESSON 10
Dotted Quarter Drill

You can tell how good players are by the way they look. Good players have good posture and instrument position.

74 **A Lower Note**

75 **Low-Note Drill**

76 **Dotted Quarter Drill**

77 **Hand Clappers**

78 **Knee Slappers**

79 **Goin' Home**

80 **All through the Night**

81 **Crazy Rhythm Bridge**

82 **Duet Part**

Horns Only

LESSON 11
The Slur Lesson

F horn: 0
Bb horn: 0

Many people confuse a slur and a tie. How are they different?

83 Slurring Smoothly

84 Dedicated to Clarinets

85 Dedicated to Everyone Else

86 High and Low Notes

87 French Song (with Pick-up Notes)

How do you count the first two notes?

88 Sweetly Sings the Donkey (Round)

89 Aura Lee

Congratulations! You're half-way through the book!

28

LESSON 11
The Slur Lesson

Many people confuse a slur and a tie. How are they different?

83 Slurring Smoothly

84 Dedicated to Clarinets

85 Dedicated to Everyone Else

86 High and Low Notes

87 French Song (with Pick-up Notes)

How do you count the first two notes?

88 Sweetly Sings the Donkey (Round)

89 Aura Lee

Congratulations! You're half-way through the book!

B-497

Horns Only

LESSON 12
Building the Chalameau

Are you playing with good hand position?

90 **Clarinet Teeth-Rattler**
31 *common time signature*

91 **F Scale**

92 **F Scale Drill**

93 **Hymn Tune in 2/4 Time**

94 **Jingle Bells**

95 **Jolly Ole St. Nick**

96 **Finger Snappers**

97 **Hand Clappers**

B-497

LESSON 12
Building the Chalameau

Horns Only
Fingerings are for F horn

Supplementary Lesson
Brass Slurs

If at first some of the notes on this page are too low, then play as much of each exercise as possible.

A Building the Low Register

B Slurring Down

C Finger Exercise

D Slurring Down and Up

E Flexibility Exercise

F Four-Note Slur

B-497

Brass Only
Fingerings are for B flat horn

Supplementary Lesson
Brass Slurs

If at first some of the notes on this page are too low, then play as much of each exercise as possible.

A Building the Low Register

B Slurring Down

C Finger Exercise

D Slurring Down and Up

E Flexibility Exercise

F Four-Note Slur

Horns Only

LESSON 13
Clarinet High Register

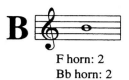

F horn: 2
Bb horn: 2

To make a good slur, keep the breath flowing.

98 "The" Scale

99 Clarinets' Line

100 Clarinets Higher

101 Clarinets Higher Still

102 Barcarolle

103 Barcarolle Again   *Dedicated to clarinets.*

104 One More Song

SUGGESTION: Gradually add all of Warm-up #3 to your daily routine.

B-497

LESSON 13
Clarinet High Register

To make a good slur, keep the breath flowing.

98 "The" Scale

99 Clarinets' Line

100 Clarinets Higher

101 Clarinets Higher Still

102 Barcarolle

103 Barcarolle Again   *Dedicated to clarinets.*

104 One More Song

SUGGESTION: Gradually add all of Warm-up #3 to your daily routine.

Horns Only

LESSON 14
Introducing Dynamics

To get a good tone you must blow very fast air.

105 Loud Etude

106 Soft Exercise   *Does this sound familiar?*

107 Swing Low

108 Mexican Song

109 Duet: Part One

110 Duet: Part Two

111 Clarinets Can't Play This Now - Maybe Later?

LESSON 14
Introducing Dynamics

*To get a good tone you
must blow very fast air.*

105 **Loud Etude**

106 **Soft Exercise** *Does this sound familiar?*

107 **Swing Low**

108 **Mexican Song**

109 **Duet: Part One**

110 **Duet: Part Two**

111 **Clarinets Can't Play This Now - Maybe Later?**

Horns Only

LESSON 15
The Key Signature Lesson

F horn: 2
Bb horn: 1-2

A note "out of key" is a wrong note.

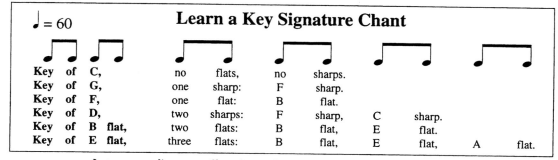

Later, your director will perhaps give you a specific chant for each line.

112 Yankee Doodle with Key Signature

113 Same Song, Different Key

114 Mary Ann

115 Etude in Three Keys

Key of F, one flat: B flat.　　*Key of C, no flats, no sharps.*　　*Key of G, one sharp: F sharp.*

LESSON 15
The Key Signature Lesson

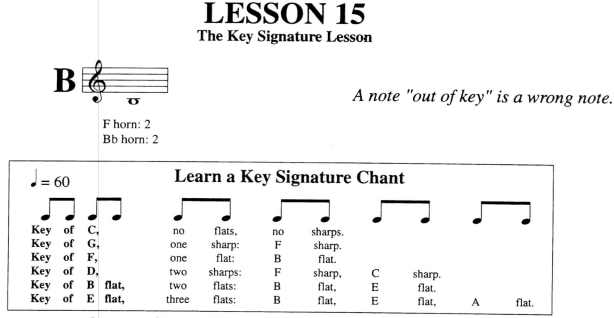

A note "out of key" is a wrong note.

F horn: 2
Bb horn: 2

Learn a Key Signature Chant

Key	of	C,		no	flats,	no	sharps.		
Key	of	G,		one	sharp:	F	sharp.		
Key	of	F,		one	flat:	B	flat.		
Key	of	D,		two	sharps:	F	sharp,	C	sharp.
Key	of	B	flat,	two	flats:	B	flat,	E	flat.
Key	of	E	flat,	three	flats:	B	flat,	E	flat, A flat.

Later, your director will perhaps give you a specific chant for each line.

112 Yankee Doodle with Key Signature

113 Same Song, Different Key

114 Mary Ann

115 Etude in Three Keys

Key of B flat, two flats: B flat, E flat.   *Key of F, one flat: B flat.*   *Key of C, no flats, no sharps.*

Horns Only

LESSON 16
The Cut-Time Lesson

F horn: 0
Bb horn: 1-3

A great deal of music is written in cut-time. Composers like it because it is less work to write.

116 **Scale in Cut-Time**

117 **Cut-Time Compared**

118 **Same Line, Different Time**

119 **Good King Wenceslas**

120 **Michael, Row the Boat Ashore**

121 **Lightly Row**

122 **Marine's Hymn**

B-497

LESSON 16
The Cut-Time Lesson

A great deal of music is written in cut-time.
Composers like it because it is less work to write.

B-497

Horns Only

LESSON 17
Introducing Afterbeats

*You must be able to play
your part while others
perform different music.*

123 **Variations on "Sol-La-Ti-Do"**

All successful players are rhythmically independent.

LESSON 17
Introducing Afterbeats

You must be able to play your part while others perform different music.

123 **Variations on "Sol-La-Ti-Do"**

Variation 1

Variation 2

Variation 3

Variation 4

Variation 5

23 *afterbeat*

124 **Oom-Pa**

125 **Duet Part**

126 **John Jacob Jingle**

Solo

"Pa"

f

mp

"Oom"

mp

Solo

"Pa"

"Oom"

Horns Only

LESSON 18
Syncopation

Always play up-beat notes exactly on the up-beat, not early.

LESSON 18

Always play up-beat notes exactly on the up-beat, not early.

127 Syncopation Syncopation **37**

128 Syncopation Exercise

129 Our Boys Will Shine (Shortened Version)

130 Camptown Races *Where are the syncopated notes?*

131 Mixed-Up McDonald

132 Tom Dooley

133 Accompaniment

Horns Only

LESSON 19
Building Rhythmic Independence

D

F horn: 0
Bb horn: 1-2

134 **Counting Syncopation**

135 **Syncopation in Cut-Time**

136 **Good Night, Ladies**

137 **Dem Bones**

138 **March for Hand-Clappers, Knee-Slappers, Finger-Snappers, and Foot-Stompers**

A. Hand-Clappers

B. Knee-Slappers

C. Finger-Snappers

D. Foot-Stompers

A.

B.

C.

D.

LESSON 19

134 Counting Syncopation · Building Rhythmic Independence

135 Syncopation in Cut-Time

136 Good Night, Ladies

137 Dem Bones

138 March for Hand-Clappers, Knee-Slappers, Finger-Snappers, and Foot-Stompers

A. Hand-Clappers

B. Knee-Slappers

C. Finger-Snappers

D. Foot-Stompers

Optional Supplementary Rhythm Set
Sixteenth Notes

3/8 and 6/8 (Compound) Time

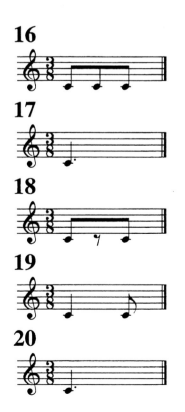

Horns Only

Optional Supplementary Lesson #1
Sixteenth Notes

A Scale with Sixteenth Notes

B Bird

C Polly Wolly Doodle

D Ring-a-Ding-a-Ding

E Scale with Two Sixteenths

F Skip to My Lou

Optional Supplementary Lesson #1
Sixteenth Notes

A Scale with Sixteenth Notes

B Bird

C Polly Wolly Doodle

D Ring-a-Ding-a-Ding

E Scale with Two Sixteenths

F Skip to My Lou

50

B-497

Optional Supplementary Lesson #2
6/8 and 3/8 Time

A 6/8 Scale

B Piano Duet

C Duet Part

D Farmer Song

Watch out!

E Southern Roses Waltz in 3/8 Time

F Hymn Song

G Lovely Evening Round

Horns Only

Special Songs for Individual Practice

Look up any unfamiliar notes in the
Fingering Chart *on pages 2 and 3.*

Up on the Housetop

America the Beautiful

Red River Valley

Taps

Reveille

Horns Only

Special Songs for Individual Practice

Look up any unfamiliar notes in the
Fingering Chart *on pages 2 and 3.*

Reuben and Rachel

Eency Weency Spider

Scales to Prepare for Book Two

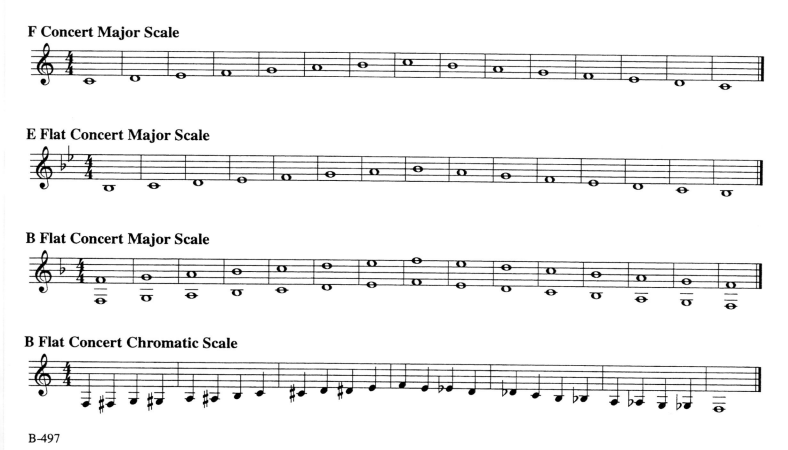

F Concert Major Scale

E Flat Concert Major Scale

B Flat Concert Major Scale

B Flat Concert Chromatic Scale

B-497

Traditional "One And" Counting System*

Most teachers of band instruments agree that the teaching of music reading can be done most efficiently and effectively with a counting system. A rhythmic vocabulary helps communication and promotes understanding. It doesn't seem to matter which counting system is used as long as there is a system and it is used consistently. Two suggested counting systems are offered on these two pages.

The idea of saying the "number" of the count on which a note occurs and saying the word, "and," for any note that occurs half-way after the beat has been used for many years. The basic idea with many variations can be found in hundreds of music books. Probably the most widely circulated publication using this system of counting is the *Haskell Harr Drum Method*. Because of its long history (published in 1937 and still used today), its expansive use, and the general public perception that percussionists are supposedly experts at counting, many band directors have adapted a counting system that is remarkably similar. The following is a somewhat modified summary of "one and" counting that might be used by teachers and students for this band method:

I. Notes of One or More Counts

For notes of one count (or longer), simply say the number of the count on which the note begins and continue counting for the duration of the note. Thus, a note which receives one count and which begins on the first beat of the measure would be counted, "one." If the note occurs on the second count say, "two," etc. A note of longer value would simply be counted longer. The following example quickly illustrates the counting system as applied to rhythms (including rests) of one, two, three, or four counts:

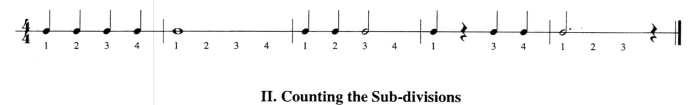

II. Counting the Sub-divisions

Notes which receive less than a whole count and which are divisible by two (some would say simple time) are counted as follows:

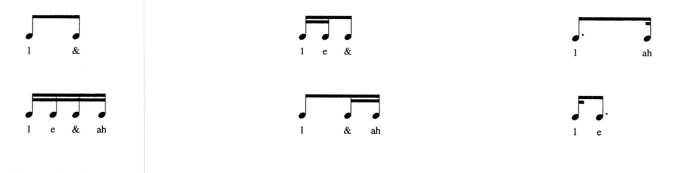

Notes which receive less than a whole count and which are divisible by three (some would say compound time) are counted as follows:

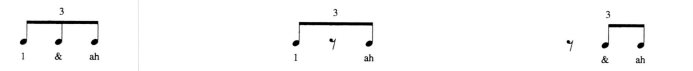

---

*For a complete explanation of this counting system, see *the Haskell Harr Drum Method*, published by M. M. Cole Publishing Company.

Eastman Counting System*

there is no "official" counting system endorsed by the Eastman School of Music, there was a system written by Alan I. McHose which was published in his series of theory texts. Because he was a theory instructor at the Eastman School for many years and his books were used as textbooks for his theory classes, most Eastman students of the 1940s, 50s, and 60s used his counting syllables.

For almost a third of a century these graduates of one of America's largest and most highly regarded music schools have been doing a great deal of "evangelizing" about their counting system. Many have been leaders in music education and their teaching techniques have been widely copied. The authors of this band method, neither of whom attended the Eastman School, have adapted the system and used a modified version in teaching beginning band classes. Both recommend its use with this band method.

I. Notes of One or More Counts

Notes of one count (or longer) are counted much the same way as in any other counting system. One major difference is that notes longer than one count are held with a continuous word-sound. Thus, a whole note in 4/4 time would be counted, "onnnnnnnnne," for four counts. The following example quickly illustrates the counting system as applied to rhythms (including rests) of one, two, three, or four counts:

II. Counting the Sub-divisions

Notes which receive less than a whole count are categorized into rhythms which are divisible by two or those which are divisible by three (some would say duple and triple rhythms). Again, any note which occurs on a downbeat is simply counted with the number of the count. The important difference is that a note which occurs on the last half of a count is counted, "te," (Latin, rhymes with May) and notes which occur on the second or third fraction of the count are counted; "lah," and, "lee." Everything else is counted, "ta" (pronounced, "tah").

Rhythms Which are Divisible by Two (Read Down)   Rhythms Which are Divisible by Three (Read Down)

*For a complete explanation of this counting system, see the *Ear Training and Sight Singing Dictation Manual*, published by Prentice Hall.

Warm-ups

Fingerings are for B flat horn

Play a good, strong tone.

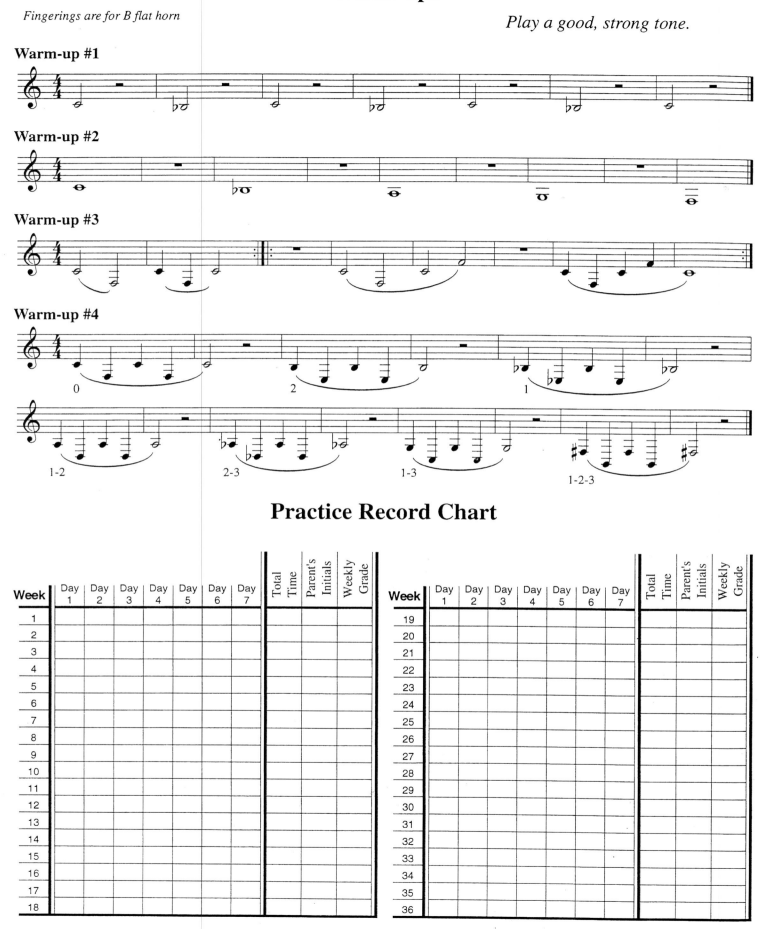

Practice Record Chart

Week	Day 1	Day 2	Day 3	Day 4	Day 5	Day 6	Day 7	Total Time	Parent's Initials	Weekly Grade	Week	Day 1	Day 2	Day 3	Day 4	Day 5	Day 6	Day 7	Total Time	Parent's Initials	Weekly Grade
1											19										
2											20										
3											21										
4											22										
5											23										
6											24										
7											25										
8											26										
9											27										
10											28										
11											29										
12											30										
13											31										
14											32										
15											33										
16											34										
17											35										
18											36										